# The Crossing

POEMS BY
JONATHAN FINK

# The Crossing

POEMS BY
## JONATHAN FINK

DZANC
BOOKS

**DZANC BOOKS**

5220 Dexter Ann Arbor Rd.
Ann Arbor, MI 48103
www.dzancbooks.org

THE CROSSING

Library of Congress Cataloging-in-Publication Data

Fink, Jonathan.
  [Poems. Selections]
  The crossing / Jonathan Fink. -- First edition.
      pages ; cm
    ISBN 978-1-938103-02-5 (softcover)
  I. Title.
  PS3606.I545A6 2015
  811'.6--dc23
                                              2015000619

Interior design by Michelle Dotter
First US edition: March 2015

Printed in the United States of America

10   9   8   7   6   5   4   3   2   1

*For my father*

## Acknowledgments

Grateful acknowledgment is made to the following publications in which these poems, some in earlier versions, first appeared:

*Bat City Review:* "Hades and the Agony of Spring"
*Madonna Muse:* "Flight"
*Mid-American Review:* "Afterwards"
*The Missouri Review:* "A Pound of Flesh," "The Captive," "The Prophetess"
*New England Review:* "The Possible Remains," "The Prodigal Son"
*The New Haven Advocate:* "Last Meal: Photographs"
*Poetry:* "The Dead," "The Discretion of Loss," "The Prague Astronomical Clock," "Coroner's Song"
*Slate:* "The Crossing"
*The Southern Review:* "Paradise"
*Southwest Review:* "Among Soldiers Returning Home"
*Subtropics:* "An Army Moves as Water Moves"
*TriQuarterly:* "The Lighthouse Keeper," "Passage," "Body of Sorrow," "The Promise of the Body Is Its Dream," "Conflagration and Wage: The Triangle Shirtwaist Factory Fire, 1911"
*Virginia Quarterly Review:* "Son's Blessing"

"Paradise" was reprinted on *Verse Daily* (www.versedaily.org) for December 14, 2003.

"Among Soldiers Returning Home" was reprinted in *Loose Canons* Volume 7, Issue 3, by the Emory University English Department.

"Last Meal: Photographs" also appeared as a limiter-edition broadside from Broadsided Press in Anchorage, Alaska.

"A Pound of Flesh," "The Captive" and "The Prophetess" received the 2006 Editors' Prize in Poetry from *The Missouri Review.*

"The Prophetess" was reprinted on *Missouri Review Online* (www.missouri-review.org) as the "Poem of the Week" for August 14, 2007.

I am also grateful to the National Endowment for the Arts, the Florida Division of Cultural Affairs, the St. Botolph Club Foundation, the Somerville Arts Council, Emory University, Syracuse University, and University of West Florida for their support.

# CONTENTS

ix      Introduction
3      The Crossing

## I.

7      The Promise of the Body Is Its Dream
13      Coroner's Song
14      Flight
17      An Army Moves as Water Moves—
28      The Prophetess
20      Hades and the Agony of Spring
22      The Prodigal Son

## II.

27      The Captive
33      Paradise
34      The Prague Astronomical Clock
36      The Possible Remains
37      Last Meal: Photographs
38      The Lighthouse Keeper
40      Passage
41      The Dead

## III.

45      The Discretion of Loss
46      Among Soldiers Returning Home
47      Body of Sorrow

52    Afterwards
53    A Pound of Flesh
56    Son's Blessing

# IV.

59    Conflagration and Wage: The Triangle Shirtwaist
      Factory Fire, 1911

# INTRODUCTION

Jonathan Fink's poems are rooted in a strong sense of narrative, an engagement with history, and the enduring rhythms of traditional form. Whether writing free verse poems or traditional sonnets or villanelles, Jonathan is equally skilled at handling the demands of language and its attendant music. In *The Crossing*, Jonathan skillfully grapples with thematic material engaging larger social and political implications without sacrificing precision of language, clarity, and the quest for beauty that characterizes all of his work. It is refreshing to read a collection that sets the exploration of our common humanity in a history that at once sheds light on parts of the past that might have gone overlooked. Some of the most noted poets of our time—Nobel Laureates Seamus Heaney and Derek Walcott—take on "history with a capital H" and show us the intersections between private or individual stories and public history—and the impact of history on our contemporary moment.

Jonathan Fink's remarkable long poem, "Conflagration and Wage: The Triangle Shirtwaist Factory Fire, 1911," does this important work. In tightly controlled and richly imagistic lines, the poem traces the moments leading up to and during the fire, giving us a glimpse of the individual lives caught up in the tragic event. Through shifting points of view, we come to see a fuller version of the story rendered through the poet's humane vision. I think of Shelley's notion that *poetry is a mirror which makes beautiful that which is distorted* when I read these lovely and harrowing lines:

> The women on the ninth floor press against
> the windows. No one jumps. They seem to fight
> against the glass until whatever holds them
> breaks—the windows coming lose, the bricks
> and stone—and down they come in groups,

unluckiest of all, their bodies indiscernible
in flames. They fall inertly, torches in the air.

This lovely collection is also concerned with the body in its many
forms—in passion, in sorrow, in work, and in death—and the inscrip-
tions of memory upon it: *the body, in its sorrow, claims as gown/ the labor
of the past, both true and marred/ where constant hemming of its will is
found/ restored in time through blood, then scab, then scar.* In his use of
ekphrasis and various personae to engage the past, Jonathan Fink is part
of a tradition of poets including Linda Bierds, Linda Gregerson, and A.
Van Jordan, whose ability to imagine deeply the interior lives of others
enriches our understanding of the human condition—the connections
with our own interior lives.

Natasha Trethewey

*United States Poet Laureate Consultant in Poetry 2012-2014*
*Robert W. Woodruff Professor of English and Creative Writing,*
*Emory University*

# THE CROSSING

# THE CROSSING

—*The T'Boli, a Mindanao tribe, believe the soul leaves the body in sleep, then returns to wake it; death occurs when the soul leaves permanently.*

The bodies hang like chimes within the boughs.
Perhaps the height is welcome to the dead

that wake alone inside the bamboo slats.
They undulate a moment in the air,

then weave between the limbs to reach the sea.
The living are asleep in huts below.

Their souls have climbed from dreams and line the shore.
The moonlight seems to fill their robes and hair,

the water moving through their feet, each step
without a trace upon the sand. The dead

expand above as if they were a fleet
of silk. From shore, the souls that watch the flight

must mark the crossing they, one day, will make.
To enter back into their forms, they wade

into the body's sleep, descending thigh
to chest: the match of throat, then mouth, then breath.

*I.*

# THE PROMISE OF THE BODY IS ITS DREAM

*1. Vitruvian Man*

I wake into the body's spell—
the hand that sketches other hands,
the finger bones and arm, the socket
and the shoulder blade. They form
the wings of birds, the way an elbow tilts,
the spreading muscles of the back.
There is proportion to its will—
the perfect circle on the page.
And where the compass left its mark
I draw the belly of a man; how all things
radiate from here, the true machine.
The man is standing as a cross,
his arms outstretched so that they form
a perfect line. At fingertips
I mark the square that passes
at the head, beneath the feet. The body
seems at perfect ease, as if it holds,
unwilled, the border simply by its touch.
And where the arms are hinged,
two others seem to sprout. The legs
unfold another pair, the hands and feet
all pressing fingertips and toes against
the circle's rim. The hips retain a rectangle
that matches with the one across the chest.
I translate to the page the body's dream
expanding wrist to arm to shoulder blade,
proportioned, bound to earth,
and silent in the grounding of its stare.

## 2. Study of a Womb

The image will not cease—my child
who never speaks but passes me, her hand
extended, palm upturned, the daughter
I imagine humming softly in her home.
Alone, I cup my hands and call to her,
but even if she heard, what could I say—
my absent child, my daughter bound
to pass from me, you without a name?
I light a candle in the night and hold
it out before me as I walk from room
to room.  I spread an empty page
across my desk and draw a body lifted
from a womb, the parted flesh drawn back.

### 3. Study of a Tuscan Landscape

The Tuscan hills, the village spires,
the fields that turn to rows of squares,
are nothing more than charcoal dust
beneath my thumb. The man who pulls
a pair of oars and bends his back
until the muscles tense—the way he lies
awake at night and cannot sleep,
the tendons tight as sailor's knots,
the pulse he feels across each palm,
its muscles stretched and cramping still—
is just a line upon the lake, a mark
no wider than my fingernail.
And what would I admit to you?
That I am just as much the man who pulls
the oars as, standing by the windowsill,
the one who gives the image to the page?
I'll tell you all I know—that art
must teach us how to see. The valley
that extends beneath my hand
is nothing more than ash against
the page, but still I feel a presence there—
a woman turning from the windowsill,
her laughter spilling out into the street
so that a neighbor pauses in his walk
and stares above to find the shrieking bird.
All this is but a speck—a window
dotted dark, the building white.
Teach me to see, the artist prays.

### 4. *Five Characters in a Comic Scene*

A man is laughing, head thrown back,
his body shaking as he breathes.  He bends
into each gasp as if he were along a galley's
rail and calling out to those who stand on shore.
His mouth is spread so wide it seems the jaw
has come unhinged, the tongue pressed flat.
The grooves within the mouth's pink roof
convey to me the belly of a whale, the spine and ribs.
But then his laughter is a bird, frantic in the pub,
pulsing through the air as men around him
look away.  Perhaps they are embarrassed
at the sound, the muscles of his face
drawn back, the skin pulled tight, the wetness
of his eyes and how he wipes the corners
with his thumbs.  His body quivers as he breathes,
each man remembering that shudder
first, when young, the body giving way.

## 5. *Design for a Flying Machine*

The metal joints and struts, the fabric
taut and bound across the frame, must slip
onto the back and shoulders of a man
as easily as if it were his coat.
I feel the dream that turns in him—
there's weight within the muscles
of his arms, his hips, the tendons rising
parallel along his neck, his head bent forward
in the wind.  I see him in the shops, beside
the bride who hurries from the church;
he is the man, alone in thought, who draws
his jacket close across his chest before
he steps into the night, one hand parting
darkness like a spider web before his eyes.
Hefting, first, the harness to his shoulders,
cinching it across his chest, he places
both his arms into the straps, and slips
each hand around the grips.  On building top,
he lifts his arms so that the wings unfurl.
Beneath him on the street a woman shades
her eyes and wades into his shadow
like a brook.  He turns from side to side,
the dust in air, as shingle tiles release and shatter
on the street before the gathered crowd.
He knows their faces, even as they squint
into the sun.  His wife is calling out to him.
Her words are from the bottom of a well.
She does not shriek, but speaks his name again,
and then again—her voice a tunnel, rising in the air.

## 6. Design for a Boat

Everything I need I place within the skiff—
my pen and book, my glasses and a loaf
of bread—and ease myself from shore,
the paddle rising with a plume of silt,
and water dripping from the wooden blade.
The birds release from branches over me,
their wings like punctures in the sky,
the angled cries, the way the tree limbs sway,
then still. The current turns the skiff and carries me.
I lie upon my back and place the paddle by my side.
My spine aligns along the boat's one seam
and light is filtered through the trees,
until I do not recognize the movement
of the river or the boat, but just the flickering
before my eyes—a pulse of sun and leaves.

# CORONER'S SONG

The heart, no larger than a fist, is not
the mythic bird of fire, just common meat
drawn from its cage.  Intestine ropes, if brought
to length, would stretch to over twenty feet,
now coil blue-pink on antiseptic tray.
As fundamentalist, the body will
not lie—all history in flesh.  Just lay
a hand on muscle hard from daily mill,
where bone was broken, set again.  See how
the thorax spreads its ribs like ancient wings
in atavistic dream of flight, lost now
beyond some million years.  What else can sing
like grinding saw the praise of organs shorn,
of body's want forever to be born.

# FLIGHT

—*The Komodo dragon was discovered
during World War 1 when a plane
crashed in Indonesian waters and the
pilot (later to be rescued) swam to a
nearby island inhabited by the reptiles.*

A flash of light, a shudder through the plane,
and then the one propeller stills, its blade
like clock hands in the sky. The whir
of engine noise is shed as if the plane

has passed into a stranger form,
a skin of smoke and flame. The voice
the pilot hears is still his own,
its wordless yelp, the sound he made

when young, when calling out across
a busy street, a satin glove raised
high and waving back and forth
above his head until the woman

turned and saw, or seemed to see,
and placed one hand against her mouth,
the other reaching out as cars streamed
past and subway trains receded

underground, their glinting glass and steel,
the woman mouthing words he couldn't hear,
her glove held tightly in his fist,
a flag surrendering, he thought, although

they'd never met, would never meet again,
and she would take the glove from him
in silence, nod, and touch his wrist,
her fingers at his pulse, against his skin,

her body drawing back, descending like a coin
into a well, flickering and catching light,
then gone, the surface of the water still.
And only now, his voice turned shrill

and ringing in the air, does he remember her,
as if he'd startled in his sleep and sat abruptly
up in bed. He doesn't have the luxury of words.
Instead, the air around him seems to thin,

and he is covered in his sweat, his body
sleek and trembling, mouth gone dry.
His hands have turned to birds, pulsing
at his chest, on dash, his chariot of smoke

and flame. In air, the body is a spore—
an image he had conjured first when lying
in a field, his young wife dozing, head
against his chest, the heat of skin on skin,

its stillness and its weight, the way
she spoke in dreams, those unknown words,
the tremor of her body over his, its shuddering
and how she seemed to wake, a long exhale,

then settle back in sleep, his chest a raft.
The air that fills his lungs is like a blade,
its coldness shaking him, the ocean rising,
churning in the air. He feels the impact

even in his teeth, behind his eyes,
his ankle bones and wrists, the sound

of water splitting under him—its skin,
he thinks—the canvas and the metal

shedding into waves.  How even as a child
he would not wade beyond a shore,
his dream of waking underneath a sheet
of ice and mouthing words, his palms

like footprints rising from the dark.
He breaks the ocean with his arms, his chest.
The fire has moved into his lungs
and when he tops a wave he breathes.

He sees already where to swim—an island
that he covers with his hand, his stroke,
his fingers arching over trees, the beach,
the shadow forms receding from the shore.

# AN ARMY MOVES AS WATER MOVES—

the waves of horses writhing flank to flank,
the chariots like boats, the spears as masts,

the arrows forming rivers in the air,
the sound of hooves in thunder, lightning in the flash of steel,

the soldiers' words becoming current over rock,
the body's voice a seagull's cry,

the sound of bamboo splitting in a fire,
the creaking sound it makes like ice in flux,

the sound of wind through clothes,
the sound becoming rain, the lashing of a tent,

the way that water rises under women working in a field,
the way it reaches to their knees, their hands in it,

the way a group of soldiers rises, half in air,
the body half in water, rifles held above their heads,

the reeds and branches woven in a helmet, men like trees,
the soldiers, parched, who cannot speak,

the thickness of their mouths, the tongue like wool,
the pulse of water in the air, the pulse of rain,

the pulse an ocean makes against a ship,
the boy on deck, his hair like wind, like waves.

# THE PROPHETESS

The slightest breeze becomes a voice, a message
on the air.  I neither wish for it, nor want it gone.

It settles over me the way that darkness falls—
a veil upon a bride.  The visions shake me every time.

I see the faces of the strangers in the marketplace
and recognize in them the forms they do not know

they will become.  The man who holds a garment
like a book across his open hands, who folds it tenderly,

a wedding gift, will pass nine months unspeaking
to his wife until, two days before his daughter's birth,

his wife will leave him, loudly, just outside his shop,
the shadow of an awning cutting him from waist to feet.

A woman buys a terracotta bowl and in my mind
I see her pouring water in the basin.  Both eyes closed,

she leans above it, cups the water in her hands
and lifts them to her face.  The water is a mirror

writhing under her, her gaze distorting, mouth
and eyes, her cheekbones and her teeth.  Her hair

descends around her face so that the tips of curls
submerge into the bowl like quills into an inkwell.

What I see, I cannot help: her lover's hands around
her throat, the way she tries to turn, to call his name

as stillness enters him, some silent beast, and falling
from the table to the floor, the terracotta bowl.

At first, I tried to speak of what I saw. The more specific
I became, the more the listener would disbelieve.

I saw the fall of Troy, the wooden horse,
the sight of Paris, naked, stepping from a shroud.

The more the strangers turned from me,
the more I learned to trust the visions I received.

There's power as the dispossessed. My name became
a curse. Now, men and women part before me

like I am their queen. The air around me is a chariot.
My robes are flames, my words a long-forgotten tongue.

# HADES AND THE AGONY OF SPRING

Poor Hades—lord of wealth and king of phantoms—
grieves, in summer months, the absence of his bride,
Persephone, no different than Demeter, anguished

in the winter, mourns her daughter's loss by baring
limbs of trees to bone and turning crops to dust.
The ground that opens for Persephone's release,

that forms for her alone the gate to spring
(consider how she's never known a winter,
never seen her breath develop on the air,

or stepped onto the surface of a frozen pond
that creaked like planks of wood beneath her weight)
becomes, from Hades' view, a mouth that closes

after her, the tunnel where he stands—a throat.
Imagine his descent alone, the torches flickering,
the coldness of the floor, the clicking sound

his nails, grown out to claws, make on the stone.
What memory circulates behind his brow:
Persephone asleep, her body fair against the darkness

of his bed, its skins of bulls stretched over marble,
pelts of wolves, all black, like night itself
beneath her form? The hands with which she held

his face (its cheekbones hard as ax blades, eyes like cinders)
only come to him as specters: heat against his body
when a door to conflagrations opens; fabric that he rubs

between his fingers, lifts to jowls and draws her scent.
Above, the surge of spring seems almost violent
in abandon (widespread blossoms, pollen blanketing

the trees and ground, cacophonies of thunder, rain)
while in the underworld poor Hades skulks alone
between the waters of remembrance and forgetting.

# THE PRODIGAL SON

There are no women in the parable, none pleased
or angry when the younger brother leaves,
none calling out to stop him, or to urge him on.

No mother scolds the father in the night for splitting
up the fortune they have earned. No sister tries to stop
her brother at the gate. No daughter, timid on the steps,

recedes into the darkness of the house the moment
when her father disappears from sight.
The only women even mentioned are implied—

the son must squander his inheritance, and stirring
in that absent scene are women eager to oblige.
The famine hits and it's a man from whom

the prodigal must take the work of feeding swine.
When desperation enters and the son is eating husks
he's gathered from the troughs, there is no memory

of a mother's meal. Instead, he thinks of servants
of his father; even they have bread to spare.
There's mercy in the son's return, in how the father,

overcome with joy, proclaims the son alive again
and kills the fatted calf in praise. The older son,
though angered by the merriment at first, relinquishes

his jealousy and joins the chorus of his father's house.
But there is much the author might have said.
What woman grieves like men? Perhaps the mother

seeks the son. Perhaps she goes from door to door
and asks the strangers once and then again
if they have seen her child. The father and the older son

are stoic in the house, this much is known, but it's a mother,
angered by the absence of a son, who wakes each day,
forgetting for a moment he is gone, then jolts

from bed and sets to work to bring him home.
Perhaps the sisters of the younger son are never
mentioned, never seen, because their beauty is a net.

Perhaps they draw men to the house, or as the sisters
circulate the marketplace the men become like children
tugging at the sisters' skirts. What plans are made?

What schemes? Perhaps the sisters, bound by love
to find their brother, entertain the overtures
the men must make; the sisters smile and nod

each time a finger rubs along their arms, each time
the men begin to whisper as they slide their hands
down farther on the sisters' backs. And only then,

the moment just before the sisters slip away,
before they twirl from arms cinched tight
around their waists, before the sisters glide,

already distant from the men, into the blazing heat
that rises in the marketplace, which sister plies
the men for any lead to bring her brother home?

One hopes the author meant no insult by his slight.
It's clear he too rushed forward to the son's return;
the promise of reunion enters so that all objections,

like the older brother's plea for fairness,
are denied. But what a scene it might have been.
Who sees the younger brother first: the mother

hanging laundry on the line, his image in the distance
growing larger, passing in and out of view between
the swaying sheets and clothes; a sister sitting on the porch,

her knees to chest, the way she rises at the sight of him,
his hair grown long and matted, shoulders thin,
but still the nervous grin, his gaze that settles at his feet?

Who runs to tell the father and the older son?  Which sister,
rushing from the house, first holds the younger son
and cries, almost in rage, "Where have you been?"

*II.*

# THE CAPTIVE

Who was I, at seventeen, who sat unmoving,
silent, hands in lap, the one white athlete on a bus
of thirty runners, some asleep and some awake, as three
young men (two sprinters and a shot put thrower)

nodded at each other once, then moved in unison
to settle just across the aisle from me, the sprinters facing
backwards in a seat, the thrower by the student manager
who sat alone, the sun descending on the fallow cotton fields,

the long horizon only broken by a farmhouse every other mile.
The sprinter named Elijah reached across the seat
and took the book from which the manager was reading.
On Elijah's right, Vermaine, the other sprinter, cocked

his head as if he entertained a message only he could hear,
then made a *tsk, tsk* sound, his tongue against his teeth,
and slapped the boy across the cheek. The thrower
did not speak, although he placed his arm across the shoulders

of the manager and squeezed—not comforting, but firm,
the way I'd seen a country vet bear down on animals
to keep them motionless as an assistant flicked
a needle just before inserting it into a creature's flank.

Beside me on the bus the other distance runner, Rodney,
looked at me as if to say, *I told you so.* Each afternoon
both he and I were sent on longer runs and though we didn't
always run where we were told (sometimes we walked

the railroad tracks that ran from east to west and cut the town
in half, or hid in the abandoned house we'd found where warped
and swollen floorboards crumbled underneath our feet
and wallpaper unrolled in long, elaborate sheets)

we never came back early to the track where coaches
(every one of them was white) all barked instructions
into megaphones and fleets of runners sprinted intervals,
a straggler sometimes stepping from the track to vomit

in the grass. A week before, when Rodney said to me,
*You'll never understand because you're white*, the two of us
were three miles out along a farm-to-market road so flat
and barren that a screen door snapping closed was heard

one hundred yards away. I had not asked him why
he thought the runners turned so quickly on the manager
(sometimes they waited for him in the locker room, the runners
snapping towels at him, and once—as rumor had it—trapped him

in a locker just before they urinated through the metal cage).
I'd simply asked why Rodney thought that no one said
a word to coaches, parents, anyone at all, to intervene.
The manager's real name was Timothy, though only teachers

called him that. The runners (most of them were also
football players) hooted *Hollywood* at him, a name
they trilled like chorus girls while blowing kisses
at him from the hall. Sometimes one athlete dropped his books

and, cackling, bent at waist to pick them up, while, miming
thrusting motions from behind, another athlete pointed
through the doorway of a class (beyond the teacher's line
of sight) at Timothy, pretending not to see, the muscles

in his neck drawn tight. While other students disappeared
midday to work on roofing houses, fixing cars, both Timothy

and I (along with thirty other honors students) spent our hours
dissecting fetal pigs (a fetal pig is almost like a human fetus,

we were told—the size and organs, weight and skin) or solving
proofs and theorems—problems and philosophies remote
enough from us that we believed they had no bearing on our lives.
The only truth I'd learned by seventeen was that the will

of nature (human, animal, divine) was not to coalesce,
but to divide. The railroad tracks that separated north from south,
the lines chalked back and forth across a football field, the high school
parking lot where student soldiers twirled their wooden rifles

carved from two-by-fours and painted white, the weather sirens
perched five miles from town to split the air by shrieking
out each time a funnel cloud descended from the sky,
seemed proof of this divisive will. When Rodney said,

*You'll never understand because you're white,*
I did not answer him (it was a statement not a question)
and for three more miles we did not say a word.
The track to which we both returned, the lanes

expanding outward so that runners staggered at a race's start,
reminded me of how we dropped ball bearings in a tank
in physics class to study how concentric circles spread
through water from the single motion of the bearing.

True enough, I'd thought in class, but force is never isolated;
waves extend through other waves until they form a net,
the kind of force that generates no motion, only swells.
*Why don't you act like you are black,* was what Vermaine,

Elijah, and the thrower said each time they lashed out,
striking Timothy across his face, or sometimes holding
back to watch him cower as they raised their fists.
What made me silent then? The fear of being hit myself?

But fear is more a symptom than a cause and when I
did not say a word, I took my place among the people
I despised: the Baptist wives whose clicking tongues spread
every rumor they had ever heard, the crowds of twenty thousand

who would gather week by week inside the football stadium
(a coliseum without seats, just rows and rows of poured cement,
each rising higher underneath the lights), the coaches
whom I heard each day as I was passing from the field house

to the track (their faces red and spitting chew in soda cans)
refer to players as the "running blacks" or "Negro boys."
The only time I was alone with Timothy was in my senior year.
By then, I'd given up on running, given up on sports,

and focused everything I knew into escape. The threats
some parents used to motivate their children never worked
on me because the stories were not needed; everywhere
I looked I saw the cautionary tales—the quarterback

who'd gone division one, then, homesick, given up
his scholarship to enter in a local school before
(it sometimes happened quickly, sometimes not)
he withdrew all together, working in construction laying tile,

his wife (a former queen of homecoming or prom) perpetually
with child, her hair chopped short and sprayed, her bangs
unyielding to the wind, a baby canted on her hip.
At school, I volunteered for everything from mock trial

to debate, from chess club to (by far the worst of all)
the student government. And though I hated every day,
I never stopped, and springtime of my senior year, I found
myself backstage—a chorus member in the student musical

(my voice a cackling hen's, so bad I often mouthed the words
as other members sang around me)—where, for five shows straight

(three evenings and two matinees), I stood for fifteen minutes
just offstage with Timothy between the second act and third.

He was the second lead (an office boss) and when he sang
his voice released onto the audience the way I'd seen
a flock of ravens startle from the branches of a tree and charge
at once into the air. The musical was nothing but a farce—

a young executive who climbs the corporate ladder
by his machinations and deceits (we fainted as a chorus
at the news of shortened coffee breaks; a buxom blonde—
her chest extended with a foam brazier—cooed loudly

for the leading man each time he hid beneath his desk).
Alone with Timothy, I could not look away from him.
He never sat, but stood beside the curtain, lights extending to him
so (although unseen by members of the audience) he was illuminated

in between the ropes and pulleys, rolling sets and counter weights.
I'd found a folding chair and waited out each show in darkness,
rising only for my two short scenes. He mouthed the words of all
the actors, sang each song beneath his breath. I did not say to him

how pleased I'd been a month before when both Elijah
and Vermaine were cuffed and taken from the school,
three officers descending on the lunchroom as the ropers,
punks and yuppies cheered (nobody knew the reason

for police although the rumor was a girl had told of an assault—
Elijah and Vermaine pursuing her into a bathroom after school).
I could have said most anything—a word of tenderness, a wave
or nod. Instead, I made myself a statue in the dark, no different

than the plywood sets around me or the busts and pillars
(stone of Styrofoam)—remains from other long-forgotten plays.
The sight of Timothy, on cue, his hands together at his waist,
releasing from the wings onto the stage, the sound his shoe heels

made when stepping on the boards, the vast obliteration of the lights,
became, for me, the image of a prisoner who strides onto the plank,
his form surrounded only by the sea, drawn swords and wind,
who even then won't turn to curse, by name, his captors.

# PARADISE

And though our classic view of it is wrong,
  with heavy boughs extending full to ground,

the throttled golden birds in golden trees,
  the lie is still enough to grant return.

As hope, at heart, is sorrow given form—
  the mother over grave of only child,

to weep again his absence farther down,
  beyond the grasp of darkness, sweep of rain,

believes her tears the only food he'll take.
  And what is there to give but body back

to ground, bold lovers writhing even now
  in primal garments' seamless flesh? She lifts

his fingers from her hair and draws his palm
  across her lips, kissing underside of wrist.

No, paradise is never seen, but through
  its absence, known and gone. The ancient dead,

still quarreling on river's shore, their hair
  grown out to snarled manes, their paper skin,

translucent bones, still weep for pasts once owned,
  and all beloved lives they held and lost.

# THE PRAGUE ASTRONOMICAL CLOCK

Inside, it must resemble a great churning mouth,
the three co-axial wheels, all with nearly 400 cogs.
Ignore the trinkets and pawns, the puppet apostles

that march out on the hour, the tiny skeleton
striking the chimes. They all are additions,
centuries late, to pacify travelers on the Royal Way.

For six hundred years it has marshaled the stars,
the revolutions of the sun and moon, the minuscule
placement of zodiacal signs. The maker's intent,

the chronicles claim, was to "publish" the paths
of celestial bodies and meter the universe to discernable
time. According to legend, he labored for years,

forging every pin and cog. So when the clock
was first unveiled and the hands moved like conductors'
batons, the city fathers searched out the maker

and carried him to the center square. At once,
he must have thought it grand—the streets spilling
crowds. Then the politicians closed around him

and the leanest produced a curling blade. The legend
claims their motivation as pride, never wanting another
clock built. And when they were done, each departed

his way, leaving the maker blinded behind. One version
of the story asserts that the maker found his way
to the clock, and throwing the switches only he knew,

swung open the dial and inserted his hand. Like a magician
producing a coin from the dark, he removed the smallest
discernable part. So was a modest reciprocity served:

the clock hands stayed, the ticking stopped. Yet a realist
would decry the story's most obvious flaw, that after
600 years the clock still works, the sun and moon pass

on the painted sky. More likely than the fable's neat turn
is that the maker crawled his way back to his home,
or died at once in the square from the blade. In truth,

he was probably never blinded at all, going on
to celebrity, honor and gain. With due respect
to the unknowable past, only the justice of legend

remains. So hail to the clock, precision's grand shrine,
and hail to its lies, the peddlers of fame. After 600 years
they both persist, a feat, in itself, deserving of praise.

# THE POSSIBLE REMAINS

Yet how many times has it been written before,
  Cleopatra at rest on her barge, servants solicitous,

palm fronds in hand?  On screen, she's harbored
  a "come hither" stare, concupiscent curves,

all breasts and hips.  Whether in Technicolor
  or iambic lines, the implication is always clear

that Antony was warrant to fall on his blade
  when given the erroneous report of her death.

The scientists relay the palace size, a "modest"
  300 x 100 feet, inside, little of the bounty

they expected to find.  With each piece drawn up
  from the depths, Cleopatra's legend begins to thin—

Antony no longer at death in her arms, neither
  concealed in her mausoleum, no asp parting

the gold like sand.  The naysayers claim the site
  is wrong, her palatial tomb farther out to sea.

In the harbor, the divers work through the night,
  their long fins rippling like standards behind.

From a distance, it appears the insurrection's returned:
  Octavian's ships circling the bay, floodlights turning

like eyes of Ra.  Even the divers beneath, ruins
  in hand, rise like specters from the ocean floor.

# LAST MEAL: PHOTOGRAPHS

The book would have me weep for those young men,
each final meal prepared and photographed,

as if to coax them back once they have died.
Their hunger rises from the page, and though

the author means to show that in the end
the body still must feed, I do not feel

the hope he would imply. The meals are not
what you would think: a jar of pickles, eggs

and fries, a bowl of Frosted Flakes and beans.
For these young men, I cannot say what's just;

their histories recede from them alone
until what's left beneath the vagaries

of hate, or hope, or love is hunger still.
I weep for its variety of need.

# THE LIGHTHOUSE KEEPER

Somewhere beyond on open sea it rains
with sky that jolts at thunder's close,
the lightning flash of forked tongues, all ships
still circling farther out from bay.
How basic they are—lost, adrift from home,
as breakers fall then rise again.

What other need would bring him back again
through cold and wind, torrential rains
and draw him from the comfort of his home
except the grip of knowledge closed—
that boulders ring like teeth around the bay
in cutting jaw against the ships.

Perhaps he dreamed to navigate the ships
to voyage out again, again,
somewhere beyond the known confines of bay
where ocean swallows back all rains,
and wakes of boats recede in silent close,
the guide of winds his only home.

Instead, he's made this little room his home,
horizon's dots, the closest ships.
And every night he sets the door latch closed
then climbs the cold stone steps again
to fire the lamp that pierces night and rain
and send its eye across the bay.

Consider how the lighthouse looks from bay—
descending beam, the sky its home.

Within the torrents, blackness, swells of rain
the sailors writhing with their ships
still cry out loud at light's first sight again,
the ancient sign of journey's close.

Yet what can lighthouse keeper speak of close?
The sailors, once they reach the bay,
already have forgotten him again,
absconding landward to their homes.
And what can stop the constant flux of ships
unbidden and abrupt as rain?

With close of night descending on the bay
and ships forever lost in rain,
he gives again the thankless gift of home.

# PASSAGE

How quickly memory tempers into form
like molten steel to chalice, gleaming blade.
It's not the past, but passing to be mourned.

As winter leaves, like boats at rest, adorn
the frozen pond to moor always at bay,
how quickly memory tempers into form.

Just see within the ease of night to morn,
the moon, though lost invisible, remains.
It's not the past, but passing to be mourned.

While some young widow waking in a storm,
extends her arm where absent darling lay,
how quickly memory tempers into form.

Concede all pride and vanity careworn
as day, in turn, is swallowed back in day.
It's not the past, but passing to be mourned.

And death is not the final crossing borne,
but first return to sentiment once made,
the tome of memory tempered into form.
It's not the past, but passing to be mourned.

# THE DEAD

They stroll in a field with no bounds
or rein, their traceless steps
in luxuriant grass. There are no harps

or wings, no cauldrons or flames.
Each guest rises equal from a bed
of reeds. One leans his back on a tree,

luminous cloak against counterfeit bark.
Another lounges in the perpetual breeze,
arm outstretched, as if trailing his fingers,

adrift at sea. Somewhere behind
they relinquished their pasts.
The boy climbing from bough

to bough couldn't say from where
he came. Cleansed of will, see how even
your mother appears, weaving a flower

in a young girl's hair, your father
passing in considerable stride through
the song she hums with no words or name.

*III.*

# THE DISCRETION OF LOSS

Only a fool would say they are perfect in grief,
the ex-linebacker divorced at twenty-six,
his roommate—a young woman confined

to motorized chair. At thirty, she labors
drawing a brush through her hair.
Bankrupt of dignity, he weeps alone,

unquietly, in the neighboring room.
Consider their lives that once had been—
she runs the length of a wooden dock,

feet slapping on well-oiled boards,
to the arms of her mother, waded out
from shore; he gleams in the abandon

of stadium lights, young bride blushing
at his name from the stands. Each night,
when he lifts his roommate from chair to bed,

she instructs him, kindly, to support her head,
remove each shoe, find its place on the floor.
Her muscles, he's told, will wither until,

though perfectly sentient, she will not speak.
To the east of their apartment lies the stretch
of the Charles, its dilettantes drawing unison oars.

What can be learned but the discretion of loss—
how in his arms she only resembles the child
who, ear against chest, has given over to sleep.

# AMONG SOLDIERS RETURNING HOME

Together, in the terminal, we wait.
A stewardess confirms the power's loss
by cupping both her hands around her mouth

and calling out the names of passengers.
The runway-facing walls are tinted glass
and as the sun descends it cuts across

the floor in parallelograms of light.
A soldier moves from chair to chair. He bends
his book back on its spine and holds it out

before him like a gauge. The others sit
on duffle bags or circulate in groups
of twos or threes. The body's shape recedes

into their uniforms so that, at first,
they seem beyond the claim of age until
the man looks up a moment from his page,

his face illuminated in the light
so that I see him clearly as a boy.
He cuts the form my father must have made,

returning from his only tour, three years
before my birth. In photographs he sent,
my father's looks are thinned to bone; he bends

within a field, a helicopter just
beyond the camera's frame, the reeds pressed flat,
the writhing of its wind in clothes and hair.

# BODY OF SORROW

*I. Eye*

How you alone discern the light from dark,
the presence of a circling bird, the lone
refraction of a reed, the shadow mark
of willows bared that lilt like finger bones.
The sunset and the dawn both pass to you.
The iris, in its constant motion, breathes.
When given to the night the pupil blooms.
Your finest veins, like cracks in china, weave.
Your labor is impartial, scant of dreams.
Beloveds in their final beds, the four
oak posts and linen sheets, must, dying, seem
at length to you, no less than all before.
How even lost in perfect dark you fill
to hold, within your brimming, constant will.

*II. Ear*

The tunnel of your hearing is the song.
The bones that rub like cricket wings to stir
the thinnest stretch of skin were anchored long
before their time when earth was dust conferred
by wind.  Consider all the voices borne
within—the pitch of song released at birth,
the mother's with her piercing trill that mourns
your passing into form, and your own worth
defined in turn by matching her true prayer
with cries.  Though words can rise to you alone
and bind with meaning all that's want or fair,
the burden of your sorrow's single throne
is held within the weight that judgment brings—
a throttled, flightless bird that will not sing.

## III. Nose

No keener hinge surrenders to the past.
When languid drift of sewer rot ascends
as fog from depths below to reach, at last,
the passing crowds, see how, en masse, they bend
in stride, their shoulders slumped and nostrils flared.
As memory rises, each to each, one man
recalls biology with students paired
and reaching in formaldehyde to hand
like surgeons back and forth the gleaming eyes
of pigs. A woman sleek in suit and heels
is given transport to the day that lies
unspoken in her now, her father, sealed
by stroke, at home. She shudders for his death
to come, the rising scent of acrid breath.

## IV. Tongue

You are the regulator of the law
where thought is born of language first, unfurled
within the mind like bolts of silk.  Because
of you, cathedrals rise to mark the curl
of saints entombed, undone in time by words
fallacious, lost.  Though, pound for pound, your strength
persists (how soon the heart relents, unheard
within its cage) to claim dominion, length
by width, of all the muscle body owns.
Yet even in your power you are bound
to writhe within the mouth's dark cave and hone,
as voice escapes on wind, all words from sound.
In prejudice you guard the body's gate
as guide both forming and divining fate.

## V. Skin

The body, in its sorrow, claims as gown
the labor of the past, both true and marred,
where constant hemming of its will is found
restored in time by blood, then scab, then scar.
As transport of release, all grief redeems
where limb will link with limb and water stir
to join with loss the ache that absence brings
and rise in making, form to form returned.
The touch of those we love is gift entire—
how fingers meet and, in their holding, weave,
as hair, to shoulder, falls as length of fire
and lips, in joining, soul to soul reprieve.
How given is the body's start as seed
to burrow, root in darkness, and to feed.

# AFTERWARDS

How afterwards a stillness fills the room.
It weighs into my stomach and my hips

and presses, palm to chest. We do not speak.
The room is fully dark, yet still I see

your form—you lean your face towards mine the way
someone would stare into a well, the tilt

at waist, your arms for balance at my sides
until it seems I too am looking down

and that the gaze is neither yours nor mine.
We never speak of it in day: the spell

not named in lust or joy that pauses here—
the stillness of a beast above its prey,

or like the nurse who passes cot by cot
to place her fingers lightly on each throat.

# A POUND OF FLESH

The heat that simmered off the blacktop of the roads
and circled through my car (its windows down,

the air conditioner long broken) soaked my clothes
in sweat, my shirt so thin a strip four inches wide

revealed my spine as armpits dripped and swaths
released across my chest from neck to belly, pec to pec.

At work, I sat alone inside the walk-in freezer
as I waited for my shirt to dry, my body steaming

in a room so cold my skin felt like it tightened. Boxes full
of every cut of meat (from porterhouse to tenderloin)

surrounded me where I had spaced and stacked them
as a frigid throne. The freezer door was like a bank vault's,

thicker than my chest. A knob some engineer designed
protruded from the inside of the door so that,

when pressed, the latch released (I often wondered
just how many men and women locked themselves

by accident into a freezer's crypt before a knob
had been invented that would let them out).

Perhaps, like me, they tried to seal themselves away.
I knew what waited on the other side—three cooks

hell-bent on making servers pay for wearing clothes
the cooks had deemed as "sissified" (tuxedo shirts

and polyester pants, a bowtie like a choker at the neck).
The cooks would throw both food and knives.

The food was aimed at servers, knives at anything
inanimate (or not) that moved between the prep sink

and the storage room. The cooks hung back until
a server—three plates balanced on one arm from wrist

to bicep—teetered at the swinging door that led
into the dining room, and then the implements would fly.

The plates would never fall at once, but swivel
on the arm before they shattered at the server's feet.

The patrons, both in memory and form, were worse
in temperament than any child. The joke I heard

most every night came from the oil-field workers, ripe
with dirt and sweat and heading out to bars. When asked

how they desired their steaks, the roughnecks often sneered,
*Remove the horns and wipe its ass and put it on a plate.*

I heard the drone of anger underneath their every word,
a kind of tightening, a binding as when threads

are turned around themselves to make a rope.
The fire and brimstone preached at me on Sundays,

(almost every sermon claiming, more or less,
that, sinful by his nature, man should never judge

another man) unsettled me by what was presupposed:
how easily a stranger's will, one's good or bad intent, is seen.

My pen and pad in hand, I waited every night as fathers
reprimanded sons, as mothers fussed about a daughter's

manners and her looks, as children tried to order alcohol,
and shysters, penniless, connived and haggled

with the manager about the bill, the food, the service,
every dime. The worst were patrons who conversed with me

as if they were sincere: the proselytizer ("Tell me son,
now if you were to die tonight..."); the divorcee

who ate alone and waved her napkin like a flag;
the lovers, eager on a date, or bold in long affairs,

who lifted wine (I never told them it was from a box)
or leaned (an awkward pose) across the table for a kiss.

The image that returns to me when I am rudderless, adrift,
that rises from the summer of my nineteenth year,

(adulthood is a force that acts upon you—even in your sleep
you age) is of the kitchen table in my parent's house

where every night when I returned from work
my parents set a plate for me as I produced a sirloin

or a ribeye (tenderized and seasoned) from a box a cook
(the nicest one) had left for me beside the grill.

When I had finished with the meal, my parents watched
(the way an audience will gather at a game of chance)

as I unrolled my modest stack of bills and smoothed
each dollar back and forth across the table's edge.

The currency, when stacked and sorted, formed
as clear a gauge as I have ever known to measure

both my worth and time—a lesson pitiless,
exact, the one gratuity of which I had no need.

# Son's Blessing

My father's father rises from his grave
and moves within the night until he stands

before his only child.  The dead are not
received alone, and in my father's gaze,

his vision marks the longing of all sons.
My father's father turns his hat in hand

and does not know for what to ask or why.
To guide his father back among the dead,

my father makes a blessing of his loss
and speaks where I must one day speak for him.

*IV.*

# CONFLAGRATION AND WAGE:
## THE TRIANGLE SHIRTWAIST FACTORY FIRE,
## 1911

*—The Triangle Shirtwaist Factory caught fire in New York City on March 25, 1911. 146 workers perished. The majority of the victims were young women who had immigrated to America. Poor working conditions in the factory, insufficient escape methods, and the negligence of the building's owners exacerbated the tragedy. The collective outrage after the fire led to heightened support for labor unions as well as significant labor reform.*

### 1. Arrival

The arrival of a dream is never as a seed.
Instead, the vision comes full form.
It stirs the way a dog will startle
in his sleep and bark at air, at shadows.
Rising from her bed, a woman dresses
in the dark. Her brother and her father
snort in sleep. Their snores, she thinks,
are like the sounds of engines sputtering.
She steps into her dress and draws it up
and over what she wears to bed before
she lets the sleeping gown release and fall
about her feet. She learned to dress with men
around her long before she started work.
The dream that came to her, that brought her here,
was not a dream of silence, but of words—
a language she had never known, the names
like chimes. Surrounded by the snores of men,
the woman heats a cup of coffee on the stove,
then carves a peach in darkness, lifting pieces
from the blunt side of the blade to mouth.

## 2. The First Day

A father leads his daughter to the door.
She's wrapped her thimble, scissors,
and a loaf of bread in newspaper, then slid
two needles carefully into her coat's lapel.
When asked, in coming years, what she remembers
most, she says the doorknob's porcelain,
its coldness, white as bone. The street's just wide
enough for wagons passing side by side.
Her father stands across the street. He lifts his hand
as if to call her back, then pauses, holds his fingers
to his mouth. The door is slow to close behind her,
latching as she climbs the flight of stairs.
She moves her hands along the metal
of the upper door until she finds its handle.
Light extends around the frame the way
the moon, when passing in eclipse,
will form a ring of fire. And then, at once,
a whirring sound like insects fills the air.
The room is thick with garments, bolts of cloth,
and everywhere she looks no eyes meet hers.

### 3. The Will to Please

The smell of men is like the smell of earth—
the slight discoloring of clothes, a brownish-yellow
underneath the armpits, collars limp from heat,
the cuffs rolled back and slid above the elbows.
Silent in the shop, her hands in lap, a girl has come
for work and sewn the garments given her—
a test as much for willingness, as skill.
The man who runs the shop is like a sentry
at her side. He pulls against the stitches
with a needle, trying every seam. There's coldness
in the room, a draft, and still he sweats,
two worms descending from his temples to his jaw.
The sourness that rises from his clothes
is like a fog. The only prize is labor—
cloth he brings and lays across the table.
Work engenders work. At home, she stands before
her husband's nakedness. Their clothes are scales
to her. The seize of skin is like a wave—
the body's weight, the pubis cold
with sweat, and even then, the scent of work.

## 4. Letter from a Young Woman to Her Mother

I want you here now more than ever.
Money comes so slowly. Every day I save.
I've dreamt of home for months: the smell
of lilacs in the garden, Sister's voice in prayer
across the table, fingers interlaced in mine.
I cry each night returning to my room.
The silence there is lonelier than any sound.
Each night, a part of me expects to hear you
when I step inside the door, and every night
that part of me draws back when no one answers.
Silence is a type of dream for me.
Imagine what the three of us would say
around a table filled with meat and bread,
with butter and, for each of us, a glass of wine
(although I know you say I shouldn't drink).
I do my best to hope for smaller things—
the sound of money in the jar, a better job.
Some nights I tell myself that you have come.
I see you standing in the doorway to my room,
but even in my dreams your voice is gone.

## 5. The Building and the Body

A row of windows spans the far side of the room,
the only light. Most girls must work by lanterns,
even in the daytime. Summer turns to fall,
to winter. Overcoats are hung on hooks, the hats
on pegs. The sounds of rain, the sounds of wind,
are barely heard. The building stifles speech,
absorbs the women's words the way two hands,
when cupped above a candle flame, will press
against its heat. The only mark of time is carried
in the body. Hair turns gray so quickly that a girl,
at first, will pluck a single strand, and then,
by end of year, her locks will lose all darkness.
Color fades from skin and shadows form
like crescents underneath the eyes.
The body's surest loss is form. Within a week,
the back will tighten. Muscles of the neck
will ache. The shoulders and the hands,
the upper arms, will knot and cramp. The work
of time is like a specter in the room, a silent form,
a flickering of candle flame and shadow.

## 6. The Fire Begins

A cord extends from wall to wall, a hanging line
for cloth, the folds of fabric like a galleon's sails.
What startles first—the sound, or heat or light?
A girl looks up from work, her features calm.
Her hands are flat against the bench, her triceps
and her shoulders tense.  She doesn't rise at first,
but stares, as do the other girls, at wings of fire—
the fabric burning on the line.  What beast
has entered here, has climbed the stairs in silence?
What will burn—the walls and ceiling, beams
and floor?  The makers of the building claim
it "fireproof," an invitation, words becoming form.
Perhaps the women disbelieve at first—a shudder
in the chest, a feeling of embarrassment, as if a girl
has said, unmeaning to, the name of whom she loves.
The clarity of fear is like a net.  Nobody moves.
And then, as if it were a parlor trick, the cord
that holds the cloth burns through and fire is given
motion, sweeping through the air, two vines of flame,
the swatches shedding light and smoke and ashes.

## 7. Smoke and Light

The body is a bull. It seizes at the scent of smoke.
The nostrils flair. Its pulse becomes a drum
repeating through the arms, the chest, the tunnels
of the ears. The truth of fear is that emotion dims.
All thought dissolves in muscle, memory in bone.
The leisure of desire—the future one assumes—
evaporates like breath on glass. And at the vision
of the fire, perhaps the words that hover
in the sound of labor, words the women speak
into machines, into the pull, the forward motion
of a needle driving into cloth, become the sound
of breath, the sound of air releasing. Light is always
light and in the moment when the women rise—
before the heat becomes a wall, before it sweeps
against them, pressing each girl back, a heat
that almost lifts them from the ground—perhaps the light
is like a beacon in the room. Instead of passing
over them, it holds, a giant eye illuminating
them as strangers, children in a row, as women lifting
dresses to their knees and wading from a shore.

### 8. *Samuel Levine, a Machine Operator, Escapes Through the Elevator Shaft*

I heard the shout of, "Fire! Fire!" and saw the stairs
in flames, the women running towards the elevator doors.
The elevator didn't pause in its descent, but passed our floor.
The bodies in the elevator car were packed so closely
that it could not fit another person, even if it stopped.
Three girls, their clothes on fire, ran shrieking past.
I grabbed two pails of water that we kept for fire
and tried to douse the girls, but they were heading
towards the windows, farther back into the room.
The elevator did not rise again, and when I pried
the doors (I must have done this with my hands,
my shoulder—even now I can't remember) I could see
the elevator's roof below me at the bottom of the shaft,
eight floors below. I grabbed the cables, wrapped
my legs around them. Hand by hand (or really arm
by arm, the cables clutched against my chest),
I lowered through the air. Two bodies, weighted
shadows, tumbled from above. I fell in darkness.
When I woke, a woman was beneath me—then
the shouts of men, the sound of axes on the doors.

## 9. Return to Me

A woman thinks these words and they become
an echo in her mind, a sound repeating in the body.
Whose they are, she doesn't know: the brother
whom she left behind, last seen receding
on a cobbled street, two canvases, unpainted,
dangling from his handlebars, the bags looped
one beneath each hand? The arches of his feet,
the paleness of that skin, revealed in flashes
as he pedaled from her. Maybe, when the fire
begins, the voice becomes her father's voice?
In dreams he swims to her, his shoulders
sunburned, pink above the surface of a lake.
She's ten-years-old and he must coax her
slowly from the dock, her hands pressed
palm to palm and raised above her head.
Her father, now an aging man, calls out
in sleep so that his wife will run her hand
across his abdomen and pull him towards her.
What will settle him? What voice returns?
What tenderness of memory or dream?

## 10. The First Sighting

A window sash, eighth floor, thrown open.
Yellow flame. A body silhouetted in the window.
Light becomes a seething curtain. Stepping
to the ledge, a woman hesitates and slips
her handbag on her wrist, then jumps, her body
whirling through a canopy of woven wire
and glass. The other girls begin to follow.
Women can be seen from far away, their bodies
dark against the backdrop of the flames.
Their voices are consumed by fire. They fall
together, sisters on the ledge, their arms entwined.
The fire becomes a part of them, a ghost
in clothes and hair. It never seems to waver,
even in their falling. Shouting from the street,
the passersby call out for help, for time.
The women do not look away as other women fall.
Some force is over them, some force behind.
They plunge so quickly from the ledge they seem
inhuman, thrown, but then there are the arms
and hands amid the flames, the open mouths, the eyes.

## 11. Jimmy Lehan, a Traffic Squad Policeman, Saves Several Girls on the Eighth Floor

The fire was at its height. Not knowing
what to do, I ran into the building—
anything to spare me from the scene outside.
I climbed the stairs as high as I could go.
The eighth-floor door was barred by something
on the other side. The stairs were full of smoke
and I could hardly see or breathe. I braced
myself against the door and broke it inward.
Truthfully, I was surprised how easily it gave.
I felt like I was standing in the belly of a dragon.
Everywhere I looked was smoke and fire.
The building's beams, the walls and ceiling,
seemed to writhe. And then I saw the group
of girls. They huddled close together.
When I yelled to them they did not move.
I ordered them to come to me, but nothing
seemed to stir them. Then I used my club.
I struck them into life. They moved together
like a herd. I felt so large against them,
forcing them together down the stairs.

## 12. Images from the Street I

On a window ledge eight inches wide,
six girls appear in single file and creep
their way along the building, ten floors high,
until they reach a swaying wire that spans
the street. The leader waits for all the other girls.
They grab the wire in unison and when
it snaps like rotten whipcord in their hands
they fall together, tumbling through the air.
A girl is standing in a window frame.
She throws her pocketbook, her hat and furs,
before she jumps. A young girl holds
for several minutes to a windowsill,
the flames increasing at her fingertips.
She drops into a life net held by firemen.
When two other women fall into the net it tears
beneath them. Five girls smash a pane of glass
while, from an eighth-floor windowsill, a girl leaps
for a fireman's ladder that extends six floors.
She does not reach it in her jump and lands
halfway within a net, her body breaking at the waist.

### 13. *Images from the Street II*

A young boy, falling from an upper floor,
is caught, unharmed, by two patrolmen bracing
for him, though the three of them are knocked
together to the ground.  A young man helps a girl
onto a windowsill, then holds her out, deliberately,
and lets her drop.  He holds a second girl
and does the same, and then a third.  He helps
a girl who puts her arms around him.  When she kisses
him, he holds her close before he lets her go.
And then the man is on the ledge himself, the fire
behind him, swelling in the room.  He leaps
with such authority—his coattails fluttering behind,
his hat on head, his pant legs filled with air.
The women on the ninth floor press against
the windows.  No one jumps.  They seem to fight
against the glass until whatever holds them
breaks—the windows coming lose, the bricks
and stone—and down they come in groups,
unluckiest of all, their bodies indiscernible
in flames.  They fall inertly, torches in the air.

## 14. Charles T. Kremer and Elias Kanter, Two NYU Law Students, Save 150 People by Extending Ladders from the Roof of the Adjacent NYU Law Building

We heard a strange commotion rising from the street
and when we looked we saw the signs of fire—the smoke
and flames beginning in the building, women calling out
for help, yet no one was around, no firemen, no police.
I grabbed my friend Elias and we hurried to the roof.
I knew these girls. I'd seen them everyday. I knew them
from their strike a year ago, but even more than that
I knew them from routine. I knew their groups. I knew
the way they shuffled as they walked. I knew the way
that some of them would stare into the slit of sky between
the buildings overhead, while other girls would never
take their focus off the ground. I'd seen them
in the market as they picked a piece of fruit by holding
it between a finger and a thumb and lifting,
like a wineglass to their eyes, the apple or the pear.
And when I tried to talk to them they nodded
or they smiled, but something in between us held them
back. What I remember most is how they'd laugh.
It always seemed to come unbidden, rising when
they were in groups, or leaving at the end of day.

## 15. Charles T. Kremer on the Triangle Factory Roof

Elias tied two ladders end on end; then I climbed
down and tried to get the women and the men
to form a single line. My friends were waiting
up above. Their arms reached out and pulled a person
from my sight whenever he or she would reach
the ladder's top. The rooftop's other side was filled
with fifty men and women fighting as they tried
to climb the five-foot wall that gave them access
to another roof adjacent on the Greene Street side.
The last group near my friends had cleared the ledge
when I descended through the scuttle in the roof
and found one girl. She ran to me, her hair on fire,
and fainted in my arms. I used my hand to smother
out the sparks. I carried her back out and there
was Kanter standing at the bottom of the ladder.
When we climbed with her I wrapped my fingers
in her hair, my other arm around her chest so that
I would not let her go, my hands fixed firmly
on the ladder's rungs. The hands that took us
at the top were strong as vices, lifting us on air.

## 16. Images from the Street III

The first physician to arrive is rushing to the side
of every girl who jumps.  He gives to her a hypodermic
shot to lessen pain.  He treats the girls he finds still
breathing, though they all expire before more help arrives.
The fire is out in half an hour.  Water fills the street.
The crowds have swarmed the scene and they are either
stunned to silence, or they're calling out the names
of friends and family members who cannot be found.
Policemen move among the bodies of the girls
and fasten to the wrists a tag the officers must
number with a pencil.  In a row across the street,
one hundred coffins made of pine lie side by side.
The bodies placed in them are taken to the morgue
at Bellevue Hospital or to a temporary morgue along the pier.
Three officers are carrying two woven baskets
filled with handbags, money, jewelry and combs.
Four hours from the fire's start, a young man's found
immersed in water to his neck within the corner
of the basement.  When he speaks he seems
delirious, repeating to the men his sister's name.

## 17. *Identifying Bodies at the Twenty-Sixth Street Pier*

Policemen stand among the rows of coffins.
Holding lanterns out, the men illuminate the dead
as crowds file past. The women and the men
all move in single file. They lean in close or glance
ahead as if they're watching for a ship. The coffins
line the inside of the pier and when a body is identified
the lid is closed, the coffin taken from the row.
The husbands and the wives, the daughters
and the sons, respond by sometimes falling
to their knees, or turning back, the crowd dividing.
What familiar item draws the family members
from the line—a ring, a scarf, a mended stocking?
In the moment when the men and women recognize
the body lying at their feet a stillness enters them:
a mother's posture straightens, palms together
at her waist, her fingers intertwined; a father tugs
the bottom of his jacket, starts to speak, then only nods.
The officers must hold the lanterns through the night.
What preparation steadies men for this?
What training stills the light within their hands?

## 18. A Young Woman After Escaping the Fire

I pushed my way into the crowd and strangers
closed around me. Walking through them felt
like I was passing through a storm. The water
in the street was to my ankles. When a woman placed
her hands against my shoulders so that I would stop,
I raised my head. She seemed so angry, almost shaking me.
She said that I must wait; I must not leave. She asked
my name and when I didn't speak she turned to stop
another girl. I felt the urge to run. A man reached out
and took my wrist, but when I shook him loose
he backed away. I slid between the men and women
in the crowd until it parted right in front of me.
I'd walked this route for months. I knew the buildings,
knew the sounds of vendors in the streets, the smell
like rotten fish that rises from the grates. A man across
the street walked briskly back and forth. He'd start to run,
then stop and walk the other way. He called a woman's name.
He grabbed at strangers, turned them towards him.
Something in him made them still, some wildness
as he searched each face before he let them pass.